CU00764350

SPECIAL FORCES/RANGER–UDT/SEAL
HAND-TO-HAND COMBAT/SPECIAL WEAPONS/
SPECIAL TACTICS SERIES

KNIFE SELF-DEFENSE FOR COMBAT

SPECIAL FORCES/RANGER-UDT/SEAL HAND-TO-HAND COMBAT/SPECIAL WEAPONS/ SPECIAL TACTICS SERIES

KNIFE SELF-DEFENSE FOR COMBAT

by Michael D. Echanis

Twenty-eighth printing 2001

ISBN 0-89750-022-9

Transcribed by N.M. Killian

WARNING

This book is presented only as a means of preserving a unique aspect of the heritage of the martial arts. Neither Ohara Publications nor the author makes any representation, warranty or guarantee that the techniques described or illustrated in this book will be safe or effective in any self-defense situation or otherwise. You may be injured if you apply or train in the techniques illustrated in this book. To minimize the risk of training injury, nothing described or illustrated in this book should be undertaken without personal, expert instruction. In addition, it is essential that you consult a physician regarding whether or not to attempt anything described in this book. Federal, state or local law may prohibit the use or possession of any of the weapons described or illustrated in this book. Specific self-defense responses illustrated in this book may not be justified in any particular situation in view of all of the circumstances or under the applicable federal, state or local law. Neither Ohara Publications nor the author makes any representation or warranty regarding the legality or appropriateness of any weapon or technique mentioned in this book.

OHARA [] PUBLICATIONS, INCORPORATED

SANTA CLARITA, CALIFORNIA

PUBLISHER'S NOTE

This book is the first in a series of basic reference texts dealing with hand-to-hand combat/special weapons training and tactics for the Special Warfare Branches of the United States Military. It is intended for use by Airborne/Rangers/Special Forces/UDT/SEAL/ Force Recon/Commando personnel.

Subsequent volumes will follow, bringing a series of texts dealing with all aspects of the newest form of close-combat warfare developed for Special Warfare units since 1942. This system of training was developed from the basis of an ancient system of fighting, HWARANGDO, utilized by Korean warriors for over 2,000 years, reconstructed and developed for use by a Special Research Group comprised of former Special Forces/Rangers/UDT/SEAL Instructors for hand-to-hand combat, headed and directed by Mr. Echanis.

Special Forces/Ranger/UDT/SEAL/Hand-To-Hand Combat/Special Weapons/Special Tactics Series Volume I—*Knife Self-Defense for Combat* is a revised edition of the original Special Forces/ Ranger/UDT/SEAL/Hand-To-Hand Combat/Special Weapons/Special Tactics Series Volume I—*Knife Fighting, Knife Self-Defense and Knife Throwing for Combat.*

Due to the sensitive nature of the material contained in the original edition, this book is available only in limited editions to certified or recognized instructors, and not available to the general public on the open market.

DEDICATION

"The credit belongs to the man who is actually in the arena, whose face is marred by dust and sweat and blood . . . who knows the great enthusiasm, the great devotions; who spends himself at a worthy cause; who at best knows in the end the triumph of high achievement, and . . . if he fails, at least fails daring greatly so that his place shall never be with those cold, timid souls who know neither victory nor defeat."

—John Fitzgerald Kennedy

This book is dedicated to our late President, John F. Kennedy, and to the men of the Special Warfare Branches of the United States Military—20TH CENTURY AMERICAN WARRIORS.

PUBLISHER'S FORWARD

For over 2,000 years, HWARANGDO has been a major, but little-known, Korean martial art. It emerged from the shrouds of secrecy only within the past few years. For centuries HWARANG-DO served as a model system and institution of study for a core of young aristocrats who would later produce the generals, statesmen and great leaders of Korea.

Certain units of the Special Warfare branches of the United States Military have incorporated HWARANGDO into their own training. To do this, they have had to immerse themselves completely into that ancient martial art.

For the first time, the ancient ideals and systems of combat are brought into the contemporary American military training experience. A portion of this training has provided the basis for this book. We cannot stress enough that it is a *basic text only*.

Ohara Publications is pleased to add this first publication of a subject related to HWARANGDO to its list of martial arts titles.

SPECIAL FORCES/RANGER-UDT/SEAL HAND-TO-HAND COMBAT/SPECIAL WEAPONS/SPECIAL TACTICS SERIES, Knife Fighting, Knife Self-Defense, Knife Throwing for Combat, marks a milestone in military and martial arts publications.

Ohara Publications

ABOUT THE AUTHOR

MICHAEL D. ECHANIS is the developer and former Senior Instructor for the Special Forces/Ranger Hand-to-Hand Combat/ Special Weapons School for instructors and the former Senior Instructor for the UDT-21, SEAL-2 Hand-to-Hand Combat/Special Weapons School for instructors. He has given seminars, demonstrations and advanced training to unconventional warfare experts from all over the world. His system of training has been termed by BLACK BELT magazine as "one of the most effective systems of hand-to-hand combat in the modern world." *Soldier of Fortune* magazine has termed him as "one of the leading experts in hand-to-hand combat in the world today."

Mr. Echanis is a former Special Forces Ranger and is privately tutored by Joo Bang Lee, the Supreme Grand Master of hwarangdo. He specializes in Un Shin Bup, the art of invisibility, the Korean counterpart to Japanese Ninjitsu and termed for modern military use as sentry stalking, silent killing. He is the first American Sul Sa in the history of Korean martial arts.

Mr. Echanis is currently studying the advanced mental aspects of hwarangdo that apply to ki, internal energy. He has demonstrated his ability to utilize and control the five types of mental, physical power utilized in combat by hwarangdo warriors for over 2,000 years. Similar to the ancient testings of North American Indian warriors, hwarang warriors equally test themselves in breaking the barrier of changing from man to warrior.

Mr. Echanis has pierced the flesh of his neck and arms with needles while suspending buckets of water, demonstrating no pain or bleeding. He has had cars and military vehicles driven over his body while in a prone position. He has demonstrated the ability to make his body immovable so that 100 soldiers could not lift or move him. He seemingly turns his body to steel as cement is crushed upon his chest while he is lying on a bed of nails or while receiving focused blows to vital portions of the body as demonstrated by holding an ax blade to the throat and other portions of the body and receiving full-focused blows with a 2"-x-4" to the edge of the blade. The fifth, perhaps the most difficult to attain, is controlling this power directly with your mind and directing it to individual parts of the body and finally extending it outside the physical body through thought in conjunction with a special breathing technique. Mr. Echanis has demonstrated this technique and utilizes it in the study of Kookup Hwal Bub, the study of acupressure and acupuncture as utilized to revive an injured person during combat.

Mr. Echanis has studied the advanced portions of Chuem Yan Sul, the ancient study of Buddhist priests in the ability to focus the mind through concentration, sometimes termed as hypnosis.

Mr. Echanis heads a Special Research Group of former Special Forces Rangers and UDT/SEAL Hand-to-Hand Combat experts who have developed a new system and approach to teaching, as directed by the guidelines of military instruction. Using the 2,000-year-old index of knowledge and battlefield experience utilized by hwarang warriors of Korea, this system of hand-to-hand combat/special weapons and special tactics has been tested and evaluated by unconventional warfare experts all over the world and the quality and professionalism of the program and its instruction is a reflection of Mr. Echanis himself.

Ohara Publications

HWARANGDO
ITS KOREAN HISTORY AND INTRODUCTION TO AMERICA

The present nation of Korea was once divided into three kingdoms. They were Koguryu, Paekche and Silla. Koguryu was the largest, at least in the beginning. It occupied the entire territory of present-day Manchuria as well as the northern part of the Korean peninsula.

In the fifth century, Koguryu made a bid to take over its two smaller neighbors. Paekche was almost overrun and forced to move its capital southward. Silla was constantly harassed. But here an unusual phenomenon was taking place that would one day make Silla the leading Korean kingdom.

Silla didn't break under the military pressure of Koguryu. Rather, the kingdom united and created new institutions to make it a formidable fighting machine. Foremost among the new institutions was the Hwarang. It included a core of young men of nobility who would produce the generals, statesmen and other leaders.

The great period of the united Silla was from 661—935 A.D. It was a time of immense development. Says martial arts historian Sang Kyu Shim, "The Hwarang entered a monumental period of peace, prosperity and development, inventing movable type 200 years before Gutenberg. It [Silla] also became a profoundly Buddhist country, printing lengthy Buddhist scriptures and constructing countless Buddhist temples and sculptures throughout the country."

Prior to 57 B.C., in the peninsula now known as Korea, a group called Won Hwa, a group of women, met for philosophical and intellectual discussions. This group was the ancient forerunner of hwarangdo.

At the time when Silla was being threatened by its larger and stronger neighbor, Koguryu, the people and government of Silla organized under the leadership of the Supreme Buddhist Monk Won Kwang Bopsa, a school of intellectual pursuits and martial arts thinking. This school came to be known as the Hwarang, or "Flower of Manhood." To this temple school, the king of Silla sent his sons and trusted soldiers to be trained in the philosophical codes and martial arts techniques developed by Won Kwang Bopsa.

Because of the martial arts training and particularly the philosophical and moral codes taught by the founders of the hwarangdo system, the tiny country of Silla eventually overcame the strength and size of its neighbors, Paekche and Koguryu, and ruled the peninsula known as Korea for many centuries.

Two of the Hwarang warriors, Kui San and Chu Hwang, were

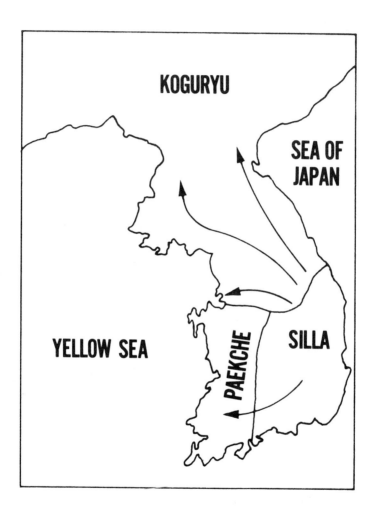

instrumental in obtaining from Won Kwang Bopsa a set of five rules by which they could govern their lives and purify their minds. Adding these rules to the virtues practiced by hwarangdo students already, the warriors had an all-encompassing set of guidelines by which they could conduct themselves properly as martial artists and as human beings. This set of guidelines is still remembered and practiced today by students of hwarangdo:

FIVE RULES:
1. Loyalty to one's country.
2. Loyalty to one's parents.
3. Trust and brotherhood among friends.
4. Courage never to retreat in the face of the enemy.
5. Justice never to take a life without cause.

NINE VIRTUES:
1. Humanity
2. Honor
3. Courtesy
4. Knowledge
5. Trust and Friendship
6. Kindness
7. Wisdom
8. Loyalty
9. Courage

From the earliest period in Korea, Won Kwang Bopsa's monastery was simultaneously a temple for the teaching of religious beliefs and a college for the instruction of higher learning as well as a gymnasium for the practice of the martial arts. It became a kind of spiritual/physical West Point for the intelligentsia of Silla. The Hwarang became the Korean version of the code of Bushido, popular in Japan.

Here, Won Kwang Bopsa and other priests trained many of the leading generals of the royal family. The establishment of the military/religious school led to the development of the Hwarang warriors who became legendary fighters. This ferocious fighting spirit led to the successful unification of Korea under Sill rule. Among the famous Hwarang warriors was General Yoo Sin Kim (595—673 A.D.).

During the Yi Dynasty (1392—1910 A.D.), the martial arts and the hwarangdo code fell into decline. The purely intellectual arts rose in stature and official recognition. With it came a dynastic policy of "favoring the arts and despising arms."

This led to the banishment of the warriors, with some taking refuge in Buddhist temples. There the art was preserved for centuries until the modern period. Much like the monks and monasteries were centers of learning during the so-called European Dark Ages, the Buddhist monks and temples in Korea preserved what they could of both the physical and religious aspects of hwarangdo.

Hwarangdo remained in Korean temples until the early 1950s. At that time, two Korean brothers, Joo Bang and Joo Sang Lee, began to study the art. They would soon bring it to the Korean population and later, America.

The Lee brothers were born in the 1930s. Their father was a martial artist, having black belts in judo and kendo, the only martial arts available under the Japanese Occupation. Father Lee began the boys' martial arts training early, training them at home as early as the age of two years old.

At the age of five, Joo Bang and Joo Sang were enrolled in the So Gwang Sa Buddhist Temple for religious and martial arts training, this temple being the current residence of the Grand Master of hwarangdo, a monk named Suahm Dosa.

In 1950, the Lee family moved to the southern tip of Korea, and the boys were enrolled in the Yang Mi Ahm temple on O Dae Mountain, where Suahm Dosa had also relocated. The Lee brothers' training continued here, and in 1960, they received permission from their master to open a hwarangdo school in public, the first one in modern times, in Seoul, Korea. Subsequent to the opening of the first school in Seoul, the Korea Hwarang-Do Federation was granted a government permit to function as a martial arts association in Korea.

In 1968, Joo Bang Lee was presented with the Lion's Award as the Martial Artist of the Year. 1968 was also the year hwarangdo first came to the Western world. In that year, Master Joo Sang Lee came to the United States and opened a hwarangdo school in Huntington Park, California.

In 1969, Master Suahm Dosa died and the position of Grand Master was passed to Joo Bang Lee. This position made Joo Bang Lee the Grand Master of hwarangdo in an unbroken line of succession lasting over 1,800 years, directly descending from the two warriors and hwarangdo masters of Won Kwang Bopsa's time, Kui San and Chu Hwang. In 1972, Joo Bang Lee came to the United States to spread the art of hwarangdo. Today, there are approximately 56 hwarangdo schools in Korea and another 38 in the United States and Europe. Joo Bang Lee is the Grand Master of hwarangdo and President of the International Hwarang-Do Federation, and his brother Joo Sang Lee is the Head Master and Chairman of the International Hwarang-Do Federation.

HWA RANG DO

화 랑 도

THE GRAND MASTER OF HWARANGDO
JOO BANG LEE

道主 李柱邦

Mr. Echanis is privately tutored by the Grand Master of Hwarang-do, Joo Bang Lee, in the secret portions of the inner arts.

SPECIAL OPERATIONS,
RESEARCH AND DEVELOPMENT GROUP
SENIOR ADVISORS AND HEAD INSTRUCTORS
OFFICE FOR THE STUDY OF CONFLICT AND TACTICS

SENIOR ADVISOR NAVY/SPECIAL WARFARE STUDIES

> MASTER CHIEF PETTY OFFICER NISSLEY/
> U.S. NAVAL ADVISOR USAJFKCENMA
> UNITED STATES NAVY

SENIOR ADVISOR ARMY SPECIAL WARFARE STUDIES

> MASTER SERGEANT
> JAKOVENKO/5TH SPECIAL FORCES GROUP
> UNITED STATES ARMY

SENIOR ADVISOR PSYCHO-PHYSICAL STUDIES

> MASTER SERGEANT
> JACKSON/HEAD INSTRUCTOR
> SPECIAL FORCES MEDICAL SCHOOL
> FORMER VIETNAM P.O.W.

HEAD INSTRUCTOR

> SPECIAL FORCES/HAND-TO-HAND COMBAT
> SPECIAL WEAPONS INSTRUCTORS' TEAM
> SERGEANT SANDERS/5TH SPECIAL FORCES GROUP
> UNITED STATES ARMY

HEAD INSTRUCTOR

> 82ND AIRBORNE RAIDER RECONDO/HAND-TO-HAND COMBAT
> SPECIAL WEAPONS INSTRUCTORS' TEAM
> STAFF SERGEANT O'NEAL, RANGER INSTRUCTOR
> UNITED STATES ARMY

HEAD INSTRUCTOR

> UDT-SEAL/HAND-TO-HAND COMBAT
> SPECIAL WEAPONS INSTRUCTORS' TEAM
> 1ST CLASS PETTY OFFICER PAAINA
> SEAL TEAM II
> UNITED STATES NAVY

HEAD INSTRUCTOR

> FORCE RECON/HAND-TO-HAND COMBAT
> SPECIAL WEAPONS INSTRUCTORS' TEAM
> STAFF SERGEANT O'GRADY
> 2 FORCE RECON UNITED STATES MARINE CORPS

HWARANGDO
AND ITS RELATIONSHIP TO HAND-TO-HAND COMBAT

Hand-to-hand combat is as old as the human race. Fighting techniques developed as warfare became more organized, and the different fighting styles which evolved were modified and influenced by the different cultures and traditions of the period. But only in Asia did different styles of empty-handed combat become an art regarded as secrets of the State or harbored within the walls of the religious monasteries. The Asian fighting arts were frequently connected with religious movements of Buddhism. Within the Buddhist religion there were both a fighting and a pacifist sect.

Hwarangdo differs from many other of the more familiar martial arts in that it is designed purely as a way of deadly fighting. It is not intended to be an educational system, a competitive sport, a form of self-improvement, although it can be all these things. Consistent with its origins as a fighting system for feudal warriors, hwarangdo includes all forms of personal combat, as well as training in the use of hand weapons and instruction in revival techniques. Its advanced stages encompass the occult mental disciplines of the inner arts.

Hwarangdo does not fall either into the hard, linear category of martial art, or into the soft, circular category. Rather, it includes both hard and soft, both straight-line and circular. Hwarangdo is considered a dialectical form of combat, inasmuch as it contains opposite or contradictory elements within its single unity, and derives its strength from the dynamic interbalance between the two. This dialectical conception flows from Asian cosmology, symbolized by the swirling circle in the South Korean flag, which holds that all opposing forces of the universe, uhm and yang in Korean (yin and yang in Chinese), are indivisible.

Hard and Soft Styles

Uhm symbolizes softness and darkness, and is represented in the martial arts in the soft fighting styles. Its power is that of gently flowing water that changes the shape of stone. Its typical motion is circular, with the force of a whip, or a rock whirled on a string, and its tendency is to unite and combine to close in.

Yang symbolizes hardness and brightness, and is represented in the arts in the hard, linear forms of fighting. Its strength is that of steel or rock, and its typical motion is straight lines and angles, with force derived from leverage. Its tendency is to maintain distance between opponents.

Hwarangdo incorporates the elements of uhm along with the elements of yang. Its karate-like techniques involve straight punches and kicks of the familiar type, but they also include spectacular circular spin-kicks, some traveling as much as 540 degrees before impact, a build-up of tremendous centrifugal force. These kicks can be aimed at the body or at the head, or they can whip in at mat level to cut an opponent's feet out from under him.

A punch or a kick from an opponent, or a blow from a weapon, may be met in kind, or it can be answered with a breaking of joints, a throw, or an attack against the opponent's nerves or acupuncture points. It can be met with a hard block and finished with a punch or a kick, or it can be met with a loose-wristed deflection similar to the Hawaiian lima-lama techniques, trapped by the flexible hand, and finished with a throw or a joint-dislocation.

Hwarangdo includes a complete discipline of throwing techniques, some similar to the body throws of judo, others similar to the pain throws of aikido. But hwarangdo throws are always executed in their combat, or disabling form, never in their sport form.

Hwarangdo training also includes counter-throws, finger-pressure techniques (more than 300) applied against nerve or acupuncture points, 30 different choking techniques and a system of ground fighting or matwork based to some extent on ancient Mongolian grappling.

Weapons training includes kumdo (Korean kendo), both with the bamboo sword and with the live blade, stick-fighting with all lengths of sticks, short-sword and spear techniques, knife throwing and the throwing of dirks, pointed stars, stones, etcetera.

At advanced black belt levels, students begin to learn the healing arts of acupuncture and finger-pressure revival.

When hwarangdo students reach fourth-degree black belt, they may qualify for training in a martial art completely different from the techniques they have learned before, consisting of 36 categories of killing techniques.

HWARANGDO'S DYNAMIC TECHNIQUES

Hwarangdo techniques are founded on three basic divisions of power—inner, exterior and mental. Aspects of each are taught as the student progresses in his training. Hwarangdo includes all forms of personal combat. It is a true yin/yang martial art. Both hard/soft and straight-line/circular forms and techniques are found in hwarangdo.

In advanced studies, hwarangdo deals with mental disciplines and becomes an "inner art." The techniques and principles are effective for such diverse needs as personal self-defense, mob control and mental discipline.

On the purely physical and technical level, the knowledgeable practitioner will spot forms similar to a broad range of martial arts. Below is a breakdown of the techniques in which hwarangdo students are instructed:

A. INNER POWER TECHNIQUES (NEGONG):

These are developed by controlled breathing and concentrating or focusing the ki at a single point. It is said to be the essence of power behind kicking and punching. The techniques are broken down in 21 subdivisions:

1. Joint techniques. These are self-defense techniques directed at the opponent's joints.

2. Throwing techniques.

3. Breathing exercises. These are learned in order to develop power by breath control.

4. Head techniques. These encompass techniques for using the head as a weapon.

5. Hand-breaking techniques. These include self-defense movements *against* hand grabs.

6. Kicking techniques. These are based on three basic kicking types: snapping, thrust and circular.

7. Finger-pressure techniques.

8. Choking techniques.

9. Rolling techniques.

10. Self-defense techniques from a seated position.

11. Self-defense techniques from a prone position.

12. Punching and striking techniques.

13. Forms. There are 30 forms or *hyung*, patterns or series of movements used as training forms so that the student can learn techniques.

14. Breaking boards or stones. These techniques stem from the combination of physical and mental power or outer and inner strength concentrated at a single point.

15. Tearing of flesh with bare hands.

16. Unarmed self-defense against knife attack.

17. Counter-defense against throwing techniques.

18. Counter-defense against kicking attacks.

19. Counter-defense against punching attacks.

20. Come-along or hand control techniques.

21. Defense against more than two opponents.

B. EXTERIOR POWER TECHNIQUES (WAY-GONG):

This section of instruction deals with what is commonly known in kung fu or karate as weapons training. Hwarangdo students learn the use of the sword, stick, spear, short sword, knife and other exotic weapons, such as throwing dirks, pointed stars and stones.

C. MENTAL POWER TECHNIQUES (SHIN-GONG):

These techniques directly affect the "life energy force" of the human body. They are divided into six areas:

1. **KIAPSUL.** Here a combination of physical, mental and breathing power plus concentration

is learned in order to break solid objects more efficiently.

2. **KYUK PA SUL.** Extracting mind power. Refers to the capacity of the mind to extract latent power inherent in every human. The mind may possess a 100-percent potential, but the normal condition is a person who uses only a small portion of this power. It is possible with the proper training, according to the Lee brothers, to develop the full potential.

3. **CHUEM YAN SUL.** Technique of putting a person to sleep.

4. **KOOKUP HWAL BUB.** Use of acupuncture to revive an injured person.

5. **CHIMGOO SUL PUP.** Acupuncture as a medicinal science.

6. **GUN SHIN PUP.** The art of concealing oneself in front of others. It employs a combination of distraction, suggestion, stealth and camouflage used by spies and assassins, such as the celebrated Japanese Ninja.

THE THEORY OF KI POWER IN HWARANGDO

Grand Master Joo Bang Lee explains the theory surrounding ki power in this way. The *danjun* area, or seat of this power in the human body is located one to three inches below the navel. It is comprised of three points: *ki hae*, located one inch below the navel; *kwan won*, two inches below, and *suk mon*, three inches below the navel.

This danjun is the center from which all life energy, or power, emanates. Lee says that a human being cannot even move one finger without the power from danjun. Although all people have this power, not everyone has the same level of control over it. But with the proper training in special techniques devised and developed by hwarangdo masters over the last 2,000 years, it is possible to increase the level of ki power over which a person has control.

This ki power in hwarangdo functions in five different ways. One way is to make the body heavy. Another is to make the body light. The third is to make the body feel like steel. The fourth is to make the body numb, so that no pain is felt. The fifth, and perhaps the most difficult to attain, is to control this power directly with your mind in individual parts of the body and even outside the physical body. An example of this last form of ki power would be to use the power to make your arm or leg move faster than is possible by purely physical means, as in the execution of a punch or kick.

In American schools, students are taught to develop ki power through the following two basic methods:

1. Danjun ki (air ki): The scientific application of controlled breathing techniques to build up ki power.

2. Shin ki (mental ki): The use of mental techniques taught through meditation to gain mastery over unlimited amounts of ki power purely through the medium of mind control. Examples of this method occurring spontaneously without prior training are the many documented cases of persons who, under extreme fear or stress circumstances, lift or move an object which would normally require the strength of ten people, such as a mother lifting a car under which her child is trapped.

Hwarangdo ki theory also delves into the study of what is said to be the movement in and out of the body of the "spirit" or "life force," particularly that movement which occurs near or at the time of death. In the region of the eighth to tenth vertebrae (from the top of the spine), hwarangdo masters explain, is a "door," or exit point, where the spirit leaves the body at the time of death. This door is called *myung mon sa hwa hyel.*

The importance of ki theory is relevant to a basic tenet of hwarangdo training—the belief that the martial artist must be able to heal injuries and illness because he has the power to cause them. Therefore, students undergo medical training (acupuncture, herbal medicine, bone setting, etcetera), prior to learning the more dangerous and deadly black belt techniques.

KNIFE SELF-DEFENSE FOR COMBAT

The defense against an armed assailant by an unarmed defender creates a distinct and critical disadvantage integral to the survival of the unarmed soldier.

The weapon is the integral factor leading to the lethal capability induced by the weapon's presence. Regardless of size and physical power in relation to the enemy's size and physical power, the weapon makes the smallest man a lethal and formidable adversary. In a close-quarter hand-to-hand combat situation, a 160-pound professional soldier with quick reactions, plenty of endurance and stamina—with enough power to slash a knife and cut deep, will be at a distinct and lethal advantage over a 250-pound powerful and fast, unarmed hand-to-hand combat expert. The smallest man can pull the trigger of a rifle. Since the weapon is our primary concern, it becomes the unarmed defender's priority of action. Neutralization, stabilization and disarmament of the weapon are the essential factors in survival. First, you must block and redirect the attack of the weapon so as to neutralize its lethal capability, clearing the body of its trajectory of fire and angle of attack. Second, you must stabilize the weapon by controlling the wrist, hand and weapon of the attacking arm of the enemy. Third, you proceed to disarm the weapon by breaking the joint of the locked extremity or simply by applying power to induce enough pain for control and disarmament.

Knife attacks are generally met with blocking, trapping and redirecting the attacking arm. The unarmed soldier evades by sidestepping while simultaneously locking the arm and using a powerful kick to a low vital target, breaking the enemy's base of balance and redirecting his focus of attention. The unarmed defender throws the attacker, dislocating the shoulder or breaking the elbow and wrist. Tearing (too yuk gi) and attack to the eyes and throat are utilized as follow-up in a life and death struggle during hand-to-hand combat. Restraint, disarmament and control are more suitable for street use. The unarmed soldier must take advantage of his ingenuity and immediate availability to man-made and natural weapons, using his helmet as a shield, his web gear or pistol belt as a whip; using his jacket or shirt as arm padding utilized for deflecting a slashing attack or whipped in at the enemy like a bull whip or chain in figure eights aiming to wrap around the attacker's weapon or arm, possibly dislodging the weapon or giving availability to restraint, disarmament and control.

Throwing sand, gravel, rocks, hot coffee or ice cold water can create that momentary shock and delay necessary for evasion or counterattack from the unarmed defender. Remember, the best defense against an armed attack is evasion and a well-timed counterattack. No matter how well trained and developed the unarmed expert is, he is at a distinct disadvantage and can count on a high probability of sustaining some type of injury during unarmed self-defense against an armed attack. Your primary concern is evasion, followed by a fast and powerful counterattack. Training should be conducted at four basic speeds—one-quarter, half, three-quarter and full speeds, so as to allow for psychological/physical orientation to the movements.

Initially, training is conducted with hard rubber knives or wooden daggers, eventually evolving to the disarming of a live blade in preparation of actual hand-to-hand combat or for demonstrational purposes during training exercises. Only practice and use of the live blade is recommended for instructors and then great care must be taken for fear of irreparable damage or possible death.

There is a distinct difference in being stabbed and being slashed with a knife. Being slashed will not induce the instant shock, the weakness to the stomach and the growing terror of unconsciousness that a stab produces. If you are stabbed, and the penetration is over three centimeters, shock is instantaneous and a wave of weakness can engulf you. Some men react differently and fear stimulates them into an attack. A key factor is realizing you may be cut or wounded in the process of disarming the armed attacker, but a wound and life are far better than death at the hands of the enemy under the blade of a knife or the barrel of a gun.

These 38 knife self-defense techniques may be utilized against any form of weapons attack encountered during close-quarter combat. Whether it be a gun, knife, club, entrenching tool or bayonet attack, these 38 basic methods of disarmament and control can be employed during any encounter or attack by an armed assailant. By no means are they limited to the knife, and should be considered the basis for your ingenuity. Adapt according to your mental/physical feel for the technique, using the technique suitable to the situation and your ability to perform the movement quickly and decisively, totally neutralizing the enemy. These movements should be practiced initially with a wooden or rubber knife, beginning slow and adjusting speed with your ability to adapt to the movements.

4 Basic Rules in Unarmed Self-Defense Against a Weapons Attack

These movements and actions must be executed in this exact chronological order:

1. Clear your body of the weapon's line of fire and angle of attack.

2. Stabilize and control the weapon, breaking the base of the enemy's balance, utilizing low kicking and sweeping, joint locking and breaking, spinning and jerking the enemy off-balance.

3. Disarm the weapon. Utilizing joint breaking, throwing and tearing, the unarmed soldier focuses his counterattack and mental concentration upon the weapon, never losing control or "feel" for the weapon, his primary concern being this one factor, giving lethality to his assailant's attack.

4. Neutralize the enemy. Once the assailant has been disarmed, the enemy must be neutralized and physical control must be maintained.

No matter how proficient the unarmed expert becomes at disarming an armed assailant, he will remain vulnerable to even the smallest weapons expert.

HIGH BLOCK AND ELBOW LOCK, GROIN THRUST, CROSS-LEG REAPING THROW, TAKE DOWN AND CONTROL

Defender evades a downthrust by the attacker. To do so he sidesteps to the right rear of the attacker. Simultaneously he executes a high-rising left hand block.

Defender then shoots his right arm into the back of the attacker.

Defender grasps the attacker's knife hand. Note he uses both hands. Defender then thrusts his knee to the attacker's groin and executes a cross-leg reaping throw.

He lifts and pulls the upper body of the enemy to the ground. Defender controls attacker by locking the wrist in a come-along wrist lock and drives the elbow to the ground.

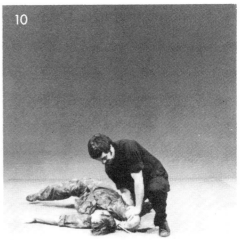

27

OUTSIDE CIRCULAR HAND TRAP, ATTACK REDIRECTION

Attacker executes a downward strike.

Defender blocks, side-steps, traps and redirects the knife into the attacker's groin.

TWO-HANDED WRIST CATCH WITH INSIDE WRIST-BREAKING THROW

Defender evades a down-thrust attack by sidestepping to the attacker's right rear. Simultaneously, the defender blocks, traps and redirects the attacker's knife hand.

Defender grasps enemy's hand. Note his use of both hands.

Defender locks attacker's wrist, while shooting the arm up, over and around.

The defender executes an across-the-body wrist-breaking throw.

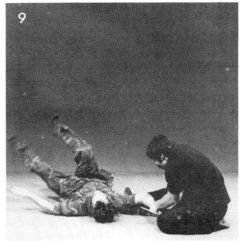

TWO-HANDED WRIST CATCH WITH OUTSIDE SPINNING ELBOW LOCK, TAKE DOWN AND CONTROL

Attacker executes a downstrike. The defender ducks and uses a high-rising block.

Defender follows through the block by grasping the attacker's right wrist and, using a 360-degree rotation, locks the elbow, pulls down and throws the attacker.

The follow-up consists of a wrist-break control.

TWO-HANDED WRIST CATCH WITH OVER-THE-SHOULDER ELBOW LOCK AND DROP-SPINNING LEG SWEEP

Attacker executes a downstrike.

Defender performs a two-hand catch, blocks, rotates through and performs an elbow-break with accompanying shoulder dislocation.

Defender pivots and raises, turns wrist and executes an elbow lock. He pulls down, performs a low-dropping, spinning leg sweep. Attacker is immobilized.

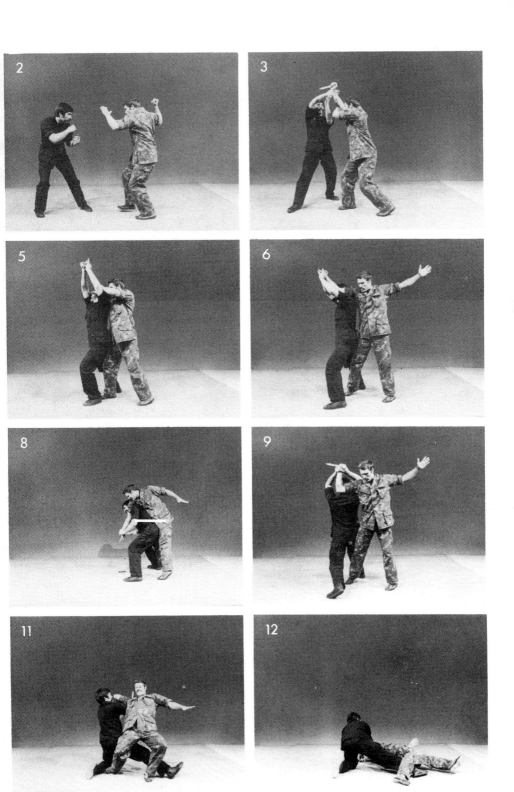

OUTSIDE CIRCULAR HAND TRAP, JUMP-SPINNING SHOOT-BEHIND WITH TWO-HANDED WRIST-LOCKING TAKE DOWN

Attacker executes a downstrike. The defender sidesteps, blocks, traps, and with a two-hand wrist grab, redirects the momentum, rotates 360 degrees, shoots behind the attacker's back.

Still maintaining his grip, the defender controls with an elbow lock and wrist break.

Defender finishes off the maneuver with a wrist twist that jams the attacker to the ground.

CIRCULAR HAND TRAP WITH TWO-HANDED WRIST LOCK, DRIVING ARM BREAK WITH WRIST-LOCKING CONTROL

Defender sidesteps and evades the attacker's downward thrust. Defender moves to the attacker's right rear.

Defender blocks, traps and redirects the force of the attack. Note: He uses his right hand to trap the attacking knife hand.

Defender executes a 180-degree spin to the rear of the attacker, locking the wrist.

With that, the defender dives and explodes into a forward roll with the attacker's knife and arm.

Defender follows up by executing a behind-the-back elbow lock.

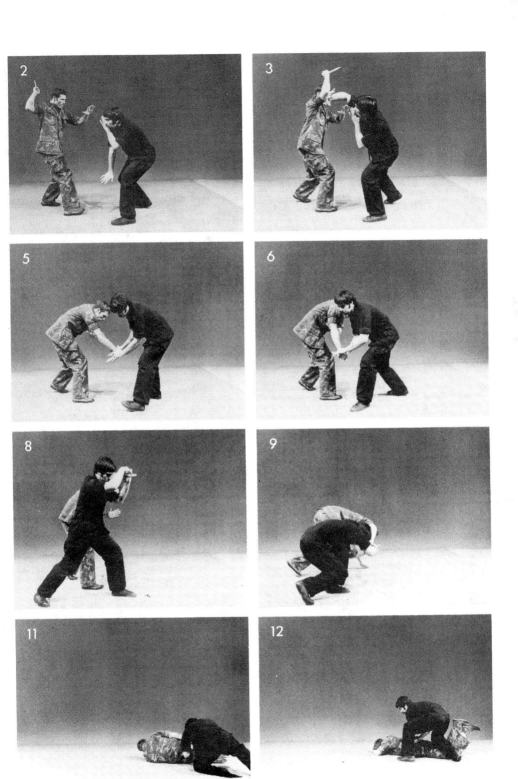

LEG-LIFTING FIREMAN'S THROW WITH DRIVING WRIST AND ELBOW BREAK

The defender literally ducks under, and apparently into, an attack. But note: Defender simultaneously blocks, traps and redirects the force of the attack.

The attacker's upper body and forward momentum are jerked into a new direction.

The still-trapped attacking knife hand is pulled by the defender in the line of force of his defense.

Defender squats and lifts to effect an over-the-shoulder throw.

Defender follows up with a shocking thrust, driving the wrist towards the elbow to shatter the joint. The weapon is disarmed and thrust to the enemy's throat.

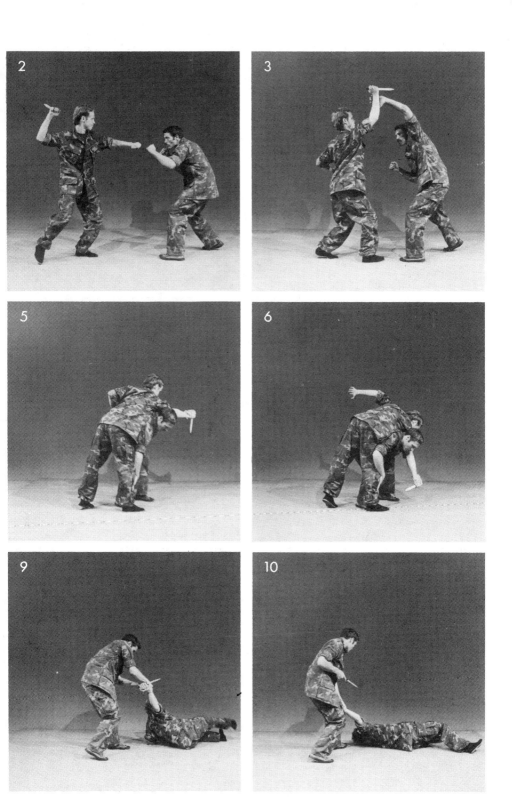

OUTSIDE WRIST LOCK AND TAKE DOWN WITH CROSS-HANDED WRIST AND ELBOW LOCK

Evading the attacker's straight thrust to the midsection, the defender sidesteps and simultaneously blocks.

Defender traps and redirects the thrust.

He traps and locks the thrusting knife hand, grasping, circling and driving the wrist and knife 180 degrees. Note defender's use of both hands.

The wrist is driven to the attacker's right rear and continues with the momentum of the fall.

Defender shoots out and to the side of the attacker, executes a cross-hand, wrist-locking technique. This shocks and drives the wrist and forearm against the elbow, shattering that joint.

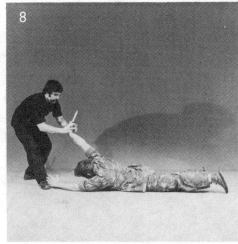

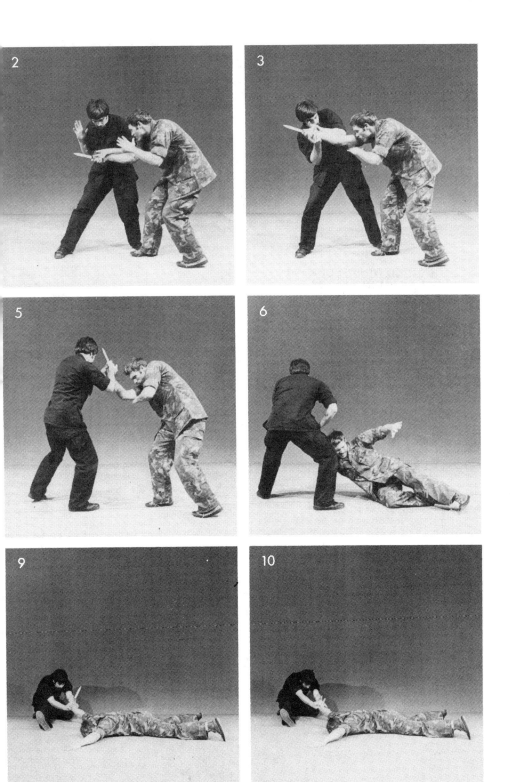

CROSS-HANDED WRIST LOCK WITH DRIVING ELBOW BREAK AND TAKE DOWN

Defender sidesteps and evades a straight left-hand thrust to his midsection. In so doing, defender moves to the attacker's left rear, simultaneously blocking, trapping and redirecting the wrist's thrust into a cross-hand wrist-locking technique.

Defender shocks and drives the wrist towards the elbow, shattering that joint.

Defender thrusts and drives an elbow smash into the attacker's elbow.

Defender executes control by a come-along wrist lock and pressure upon the nerve center directly above the elbow.

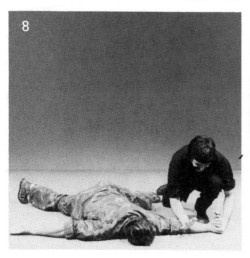

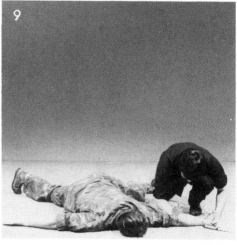

45

TWO-HANDED WRIST CATCH WITH BODY-DROPPING ELBOW BREAK

By sidestepping to the right rear of the attacker, the defender evades a right-hand straight thrust to his mid-section.

He simultaneously blocks, traps and redirects the force of the blow by grasping the wrist in a two-hand, thumbs-crossed hold, jerking and pulling.

The defender rotates the attacking knife hand, locking the elbow into his arm pit.

Defender then executes a back-dropping fall, focusing his weight upon the area directly above the elbow and driving the enemy's head and shoulder into the ground.

Defender breaks the attacker's elbow, dislocates the shoulder and renders the enemy unconscious.

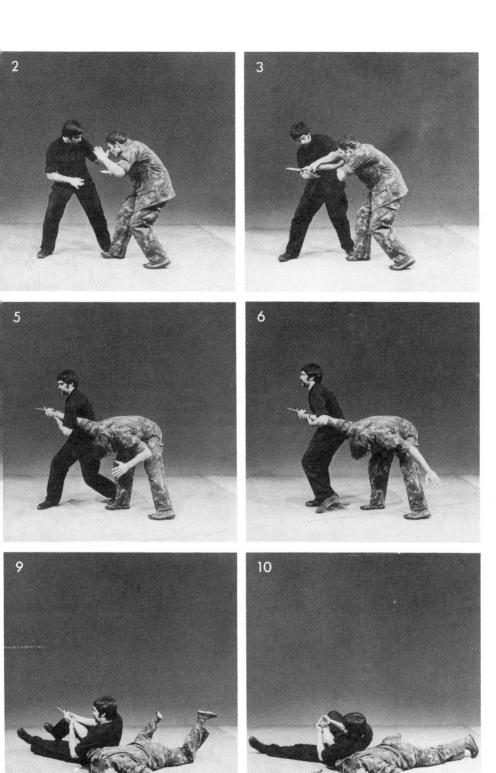

47

CROSS-HANDED WRIST LOCK, DRIVING ELBOW BREAK WITH SNAPPING HEAD KICK

Evading a straight right-hand thrust to the midsection, the defender sidesteps to the attacker's right rear. He then blocks, traps and redirects the force of the blow of the attacker's right hand.

Defender grasps with two hands, steps, jerks and pulls 180 degrees to his rear, locking the wrist, shocking and driving the wrist towards the elbow and shattering that joint.

Defender then executes a snapping, thrusting front kick to the attacker's face.

ACROSS-THE-BODY ELBOW LOCK WITH DROPPING SHOULDER THROW

Defender evades the attacker's thrusting right hand by sidestepping to the right rear of the attacker and blocking as he does so.

Defender traps and redirects the thrusting knife hand, controls the wrist and weapon.

Defender jerks and pulls the elbow across the chest of his own body, thrusting his left arm and shoulder upward and out—breaking the attacker's elbow.

Stepping in and grasping the hair of the attacker, the defender executes a dropping shoulder throw. This is followed up by breaking the elbow over the knee.

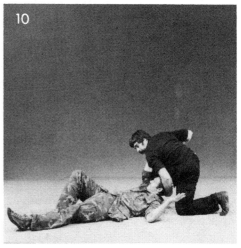

ELBOW-BREAKING SHOULDER THROW

Defender evades a right-hand straight thrust by backstepping and sidestepping the attacking knife hand.

He simultaneously blocks, traps and redirects the thrusting knife hand. Grasping the wrist with both hands, the defender jerks and pulls the attacker's arm in an upward and outward motion.

Defender then shoots in and under the elbow of the attacker. Rotating and locking the elbow of the attacker, he squats into position to execute a shoulder throw.

Defender then thrusts his body upward, breaking the elbow and dislocating the shoulder as he executes a shoulder throw.

53

TWO-HANDED BACK-THRUSTING WRIST LOCK, GROIN KICK AND STOMACH THROW

Evading the attacker's right-hand thrust to his midsection, the defender simultaneously blocks, traps and redirects the attack by grasping the wrist with both hands, sidestepping and applying a wrist lock.

Defender thrusts the knife and the wrist back into the body of the attacker.

Defender then executes a snapping, thrusting groin kick into the attacker.

Defender next launches a stomach throw, executed by thrusting the knife hand toward the body of the attacker as it is tossed over him.

ACROSS, OVER AND UNDER ELBOW LOCK WITH LEG-SWEEPING TAKE DOWN AND BODY-DROP ELBOW BREAK

Evading a left-handed, straight thrust, the defender sidesteps to the attacker's right rear while blocking, trapping and redirecting with his left hand.

Defender jerks, pulls and thrusts the knife toward the attacker's front. He then shoots his right hand to the inside of the attacker's body, wrapping and locking the elbow.

At the same time, he executes a crossover and under-elbow lock against the attacker; he then thrusts his elbow into the floating ribs of the attacker and sweeps the left lead leg of the attacker.

Defender drives the wrist and elbow down toward the shoulder while executing a dropping elbow break.

TWO-HANDED WRIST LOCK WITH LEG-DROPPING ELBOW LOCK AND SCISSORING BREAK

Defender evades a right-hand straight thrust by backstepping and sidestepping the oncoming thrust. At the same time, the defender blocks, traps and redirects the attack.

The defender graps the wrist with his two hands and executes a cross-hand wrist-locking technique. Defender jerks and pulls, rotating the attacker's elbow.

The defender then executes an elbow break by shooting his right leg over the extended arm of the attacker, then twisting and shocking the elbow in a scissor-like movement.

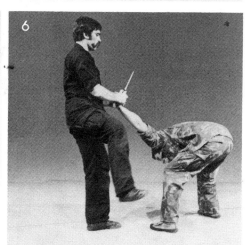

TWO-HANDED WRIST LOCK AND ELBOW LOCK WITH ACROSS-THE-BODY TRIPPING THROW

The defender evades a right-hand straight thrust to his midsection by side-stepping and simultaneously blocking, trapping and redirecting the thrust of the attacker.

Defender grasps attacker's wrist, using two hands. Rotating and jerk-

ing, he pulls the elbow into the crook of his upper arm and forearm.

The defender then executes a 180-degree spin to his right rear, breaking the attacker's elbow and dislocating his shoulder as he throws his enemy over his extended leg.

CROSS-BLOCK AND ELBOW LOCK WITH SPINNING TAKE DOWN

When the attacker launches an upward thrust, the defender executes a cross-block and elbow lock, spinning 260 degrees to the rear and side, thrusting the shoulder and head of the attacker into the ground while simultaneously breaking the elbow.

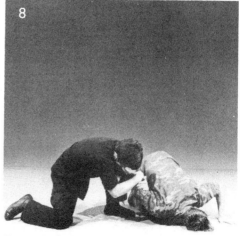

INSIDE
SPINNING GROIN THRUST

Attacker slashes at the defender's head. The defender eludes the slash by ducking, then steps toward the knife.

Defender executes a two-hand wrist-grab, rotates and redirects the knife into the attacker's groin.

OUTSIDE WRIST LOCK, PALM HEEL STRIKE, CROSS-LEG REAPING THROW WITH KNEE-DROPPING ELBOW BREAK

Attacker slashes at the head. The defender executes a high-rising, outside block, while sidestepping to the attacker's left rear.

The defender executes an open-palm heel strike to the throat and chin of the attacker.

Defender follows this with an outside wrist lock and cross-leg reaping throw.

Attacker is dropped to the ground. Defender breaks the elbow of the attacker and tears his throat.

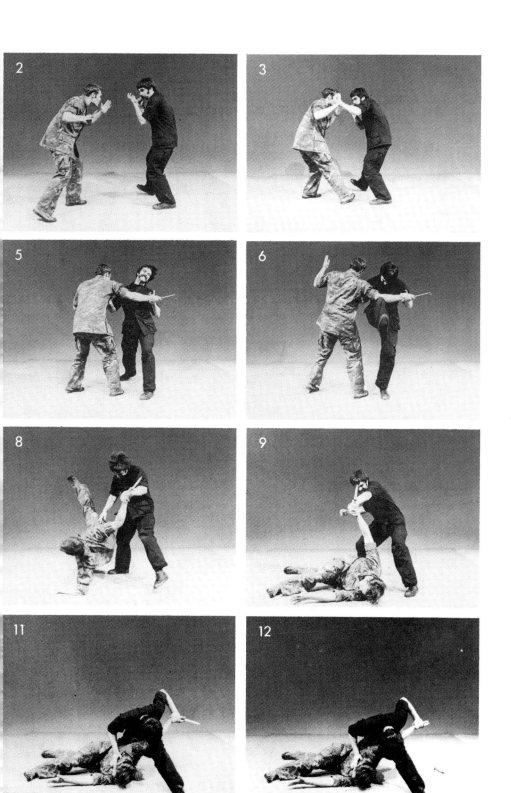

LOW-DROPPING SHOULDER THROW WITH ROLLING SPINNING WRIST BREAK

The attacker slashes at the head. The defender blocks, grasps the wrist with both hands, rotates counter-clockwise, dropping to one knee, and executes a dropping, floating, over-the-shoulder throw.

Defender then executes a two-handed wrist lock, rotating, spinning and turning 360 degrees to the out-side of the attacker.

Defender concludes by breaking the attacker's wrist and disarming the weapon.

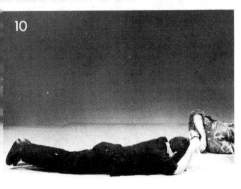

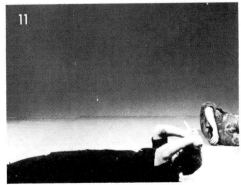

SLASHING
TRAP WITH ELBOW CATCH,
COME-ALONG HAND TECHNIQUE

Defender evades attacker's right-handed, slashing move by sidestepping to the attacker's right rear. He thus covers and protects his groin and lower portion of his body. Defender's right arm, elbow and shoulder simultaneously cover the inside portion of his head and face to avoid the blade, returning in the same slash trajectory as just executed.

Defender rotates his body into the body of the attacker, simultaneously blocking, trapping and redirecting the attacker's arm.

Defender locks the attacker's wrist with a circular, shocking motion into a come-along wrist control.

Defender also shatters the attacker's wrist and elbow with a shocking thrust motion back toward the attacker's elbow.

SLASHING TRAP WITH SCISSORING ELBOW BREAK, LEG SWEEP AND FOLLOW-UP

Defender evades the attacker's slash by sidestepping to the left rear of the attacker.

As the knife returns in its trajectory, the defender catches, traps, blocks and breaks the elbow in a shocking, scissoring movement.

This move is executed between the defender's two forearms.

Defender then executes a lead leg shin kick and leg sweep, turning 180 degrees for the follow-up.

BACK-SPINNING CROSS-BLOCK AND ELBOW LOCK WITH A SPINNING TAKE DOWN

The defender evades the attack from the rear by sidestepping and moving to the left.

Spinning 180 degrees, the defender simultaneously blocks, traps and redirects the thrust of the attacker.

He executes a two-handed elbow lock while shooting across the attacker's front.

The defender spins and rotates 180 degrees to the right rear of the attacker, driving the elbow and head into the ground while breaking the elbow.

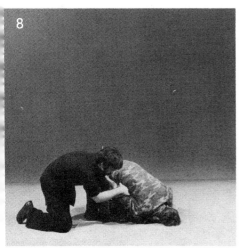

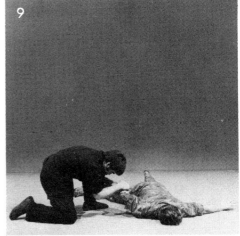

BACK-SPINNING GROIN THRUST

The defender evades the attack from the rear by sidestepping directly to the left of the attacker.

He simultaneously blocks, traps and redirects the attacking knife hand with his left hand.

The defender then executes a two-handed wrist lock while lifting the attacking arm up, around and over the defender's head and executing a 180-degree spin to the back of the attacker.

The defender thrusts the blade into the groin of the enemy.

BACK-SPINNING
INSIDE TWO-HANDED
WRIST-BREAKING THROW

The defender evades the knife attack from the rear by sidestepping to the direct right of the attacker. He simultaneously locks, traps and redirects the attacking knife hand.

He then performs a two-handed wrist lock, lifting the arm up, over and around while shooting across the front of the attacker.

The defender then pulls, drops and breaks the attacker's wrist while throwing him to the ground.

BACK-SPINNING OUTSIDE TWO-HANDED WRIST-BREAKING THROW

The defender evades the knife attack from the rear by sidestepping to the direct left of the attacker while simultaneously blocking, trapping and redirecting the attacking knife hand.

He then executes a two-handed wrist grab while lifting, turning and pulling.

The defender spins 180 degrees to the right rear of the attacker while throwing the enemy and breaking the wrist.

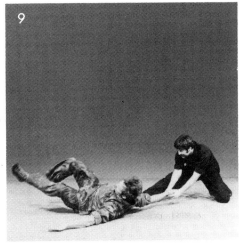

BACK-SPINNING CROSS-HANDED WRIST LOCK WITH STRIKING ELBOW BREAK

The defender evades the knife attack from the rear by sidestepping to the direct right of the attacker while simultaneously blocking, trapping and redirecting the attacking knife hand.

He then executes a cross-hand wrist-locking technique, spinning 180 degrees to the attacker's rear.

The defender then executes a thrusting elbow smash directly above the elbow joint as he rotates and locks for the thrust to the ground.

He then applies a come-along wrist control while driving the elbow into the ground.

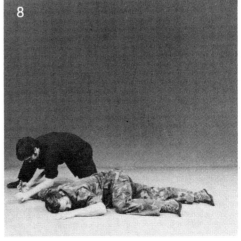

BACK-SPINNING CROSS-HANDED WRIST LOCK WITH SNAPPING HEAD KICK

The defender evades the knife attack from the rear by sidestepping to the right of the attacker while simultaneously locking, trapping and redirecting the attacking knife hand.

He executes a two-handed, cross-handed, wrist-locking technique.

The defender then executes a shocking, driving, thrusting motion of the wrist towards the elbow, shattering the joint.

He then executes a snapping, thrusting front kick to the enemy's face.

BACK-SPINNING OUTSIDE TWO-HANDED WRIST LOCK WITH CROSS-LEG REAPING THROW

The defender evades the knife attack from the rear by sidestepping to the right of the attacker while simultaneously blocking, trapping and redirecting the attacking knife hand.

He executes a two-handed outside wrist-locking technique while rotating 180 degrees to the attacker's front.

The defender pulls and jerks the attacking knife hand to the front as the attacker pulls back.

He rotates 180 degrees to the rear of the attacker and simultaneously locks the wrist in a two-handed outside wrist-locking technique executed in conjunction with a cross-leg reaping throw.

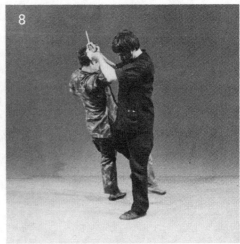

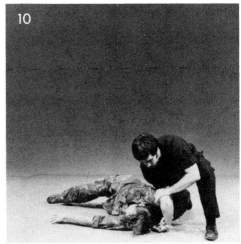

A BACK-SPINNING ELBOW LOCK WITH ACROSS-THE-BODY TRIPPING THROW

The defender evades the knife attack from the rear by sidestepping to the direct right of the attacker while blocking, trapping and redirecting the attacking knife hand.

He performs a two-handed wrist-locking technique while catching the attacker's elbow in the crook of the elbow and upper arm.

The defender executes a 360-degree spin to his right rear, breaking the elbow, dislocating the shoulder and throwing the enemy over the extended leg of the defender.

BACK-SPINNING SHOOT-BEHIND AND ELBOW LOCK WITH WRIST-BREAKING TAKE DOWN

The defender evades the knife attack from the rear by sidestepping directly to the left side of the attacker while simultaneously blocking, trapping and redirecting the attacking knife hand.

He executes a two-handed wrist grab while shooting directly across the attacker's front.

The defender lifts, jumps, spins and rotates 360 degrees to the enemy's rear.

He then rotates the wrist while stepping back and throws the enemy to the ground while executing a rotating wrist-break technique.

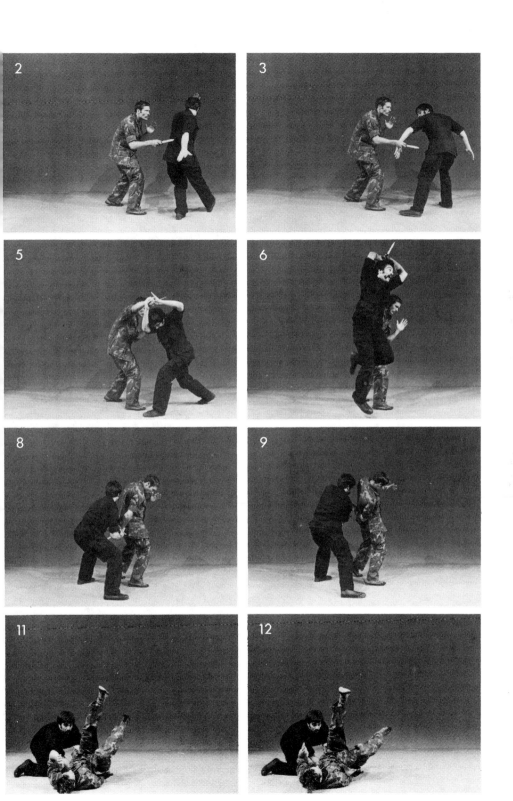

BACK-SPINNING ELBOW LOCK AND SHOULDER THROW

The defender evades the knife attack from the rear by sidestepping to the direct right of the attacker while simultaneously blocking, trapping and redirecting the attacking knife hand.

He executes a two-handed wrist grab while shooting directly underneath the attacker's elbow and shoulder, squatting and preparing for an upward thrust of the shoulder and a downward pull of the arm.

The defender breaks the elbow, dislocates the shoulder and executes a shoulder throw, disarming the enemy and follows up with a downward thrust to the body.

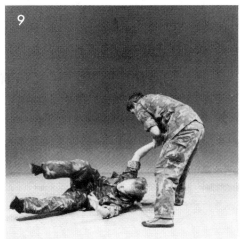

SIDESTEPPING INSIDE CRESCENT KICK

The knife attacker steps forward, thrusting to the midsection of the defender. The defender sidesteps to his right and to the enemy's direct

left. He then performs an inside crescent kick, striking the handle of the weapon and dislodging it from the enemy's hands.

SIDESTEPPING OUTSIDE CRESCENT KICK

The knife attacker thrusts to the midsection of the defender. The defender sidesteps to his immediate left and to the attacker's direct right. He then chambers his leg and performs an outside crescent kick to the back

of the hand and handle of the blade, dislodging it from the enemy. Note: at this point the defender is ready to execute any number of unarmed attacks, including multiple kicks.

HIGH-RISING
SNAPPING SIDE KICK

The attacker thrusts towards the head and eyes of the defender. The defender evades by dropping his body back while simultaneously cocking and chambering his right lead leg. He executes a

rising side kick to the hand and handle of the weapon. He immediately retracts the right leg with an availability of innumerable multiple kicking techniques.

DROPPING SIDE KICK

The defender assumes a ready mobile position as the attacker thrusts towards the head of the defender. He evades by dropping to the ground; then springing off with his feet and hands, he executes a thrusting side kick, either to the wrist,

elbow or arm pit of the attacker. Note: the defender at this point can either sweep the lead right leg of the enemy with his left leg, execute a leg scissoring technique or perform multiple kicks from the down position.

CONCLUSION

In the study of unconventional warfare, the paramilitary operative is expected to remain and survive for extended periods of time behind enemy lines, sometimes isolated and alone. The discipline and psychological stability required to outstay the enemy for extended periods of time in his own environment can be developed and maintained only after countless hours of training and a lifelong commitment to self-discipline; not the mass-produced item of the divisional training camps, but the individually selected soldier who is willing to devote his life to the elite of the professional soldiers.

There is no substitute for the most expensive commodity of them all—progressive combat-oriented training, leading to a well-trained combat-oriented soldier. By progressive we mean the constant individual and team progression towards excellence, as each training session leads each individual member closer to perfect timing and reaction and we begin to create a fine-tuned fighting machine. We are only as strong as the weakest man within our team; therefore, it is the responsibility of the individual soldier to test himself constantly and strive for perfection. The very essence of special warfare training should be orientation towards the psychological/physical combat-readiness of the individual soldier, not the battalions on paper but highly trained, highly motivated, individual professional soldiers working together as a team.

Please bear in mind that the study of hand-to-hand combat has been used as the basis of discipline in the training of warriors since the warrior class was created.

Hand-to-hand combat can be utilized as a form of self-improvement, a competitive sport or as an educational system, but never losing the context of its objective and, therefore, training is always executed in its combat form. It can be a means of utilizing the most basic physical training programs and directing them towards combat-readiness, giving the individual soldier a needed change of routine and instilling a sense of self-confidence through increased physical ability and mental alertness, leading to a true fighting spirit.

In the elite Special Warfare units of the military, it is essential that every individual soldier be in a state of 24-hour combat-readiness; therefore, he must maintain the highest physical and mental standards of excellence. Only through a lifelong dedication to a way of life and a form of discipline can one expect to achieve these high standards of professionalism. For every man who enters the elite with the ideal of being the best, these goals and standards must apply.

Hopefully, the study conducted by this Research Group has led us to an effective system for the development of programs to instill these virtues. This is the first basic study on this subject matter and by no means does this imply that it is a complete study of the psychological/physical results of hand-to-hand combat training and its effects on the individual soldier and its relationship to the overall combat-readiness of the Special Warfare units concerned, but only as a basis of understanding, so that every man who reads this book may search within himself to discover, through his own ingenuity and creative ability, techniques that will adapt to the situation and conform to his psychological/physical needs.

Future volumes will deal with advanced fighting systems, oriented towards the mastery of the knife and other weapons as needed for combat use.

STUDY GROUP A
Office of Research & Development
Director of Psycho-Physical Studies

—Michael D. Echanis